TNT

Tips and Techniques

Dynamic Ways to Reward,
Energize &
Motivate Your Teams

Gregory P. Smith

Chart Your Course Publications
Conyers, Georgia

TNT

Second Edition
Copyright © 2000 by Gregory P. Smith

Chart Your Course Publications
2814 Hwy SW
Conyers, Georgia 30094

For a list of other publications or for more information, please call (800) 821-2487. In Alaska, Hawaii and internationally please call (770) 860-9464 or visit http://www.ChartCourse.com

Smith, Gregory P.
TNT: Dynamic Ideas to Reward, Energize and Motivate Your Teams
Pages: 77

ISBN: 9676843-0-7
Printed in the United States of America

TNT
TABLE OF CONTENTS

INTRODUCTION:

CREATING A DYNAMIC WORK PLACE

Today's workplace is different, diverse, and constantly changing. The typical employer/employee relationship of old has been turned upside down. The combination of almost limitless job opportunities and less reward for employee loyalty has created an environment where the business needs its employees more than the employees need the business. The winners of today's business economy is one that can create a work environment that attracts, keeps and motivates its workforce to high levels of productivity.

Just like the Titanic, today's mobile employees jump ship for as little as a $1.00 hr raise.

Just like the Titanic, today's mobile employees jump ship for as little as a $1.00 hr raise. Because it is so difficult to find help, the main issue today is not finding, but *keeping* the workforce you have. Supervisors and managers who maximize the potential, creative abilities and talents of the entire workforce have a greater competitive advantage than those who don't. Motivated workers provide the health insurance businesses desperately needed in these chaotic times.

HOW TO MOTIVATE PEOPLE--THE PRIDE SYSTEM

Supervisors have the responsibility for creating a motivating working environment. Dr. Edwards Deming said, "The aim of leadership should be to improve the performance of man and machine, to improve quality, to increase output, and simultaneously to bring pride of workmanship to people." A motivating environment is one that gives workers a sense of pride in what they do. To show supervisors and managers how to build a more productive work environment, I've created a five-step process called the PRIDE system. Leaders can improve motivation within their organizations by following this process:

- Provide a positive working environment
- Recognize, reward, reinforce the right behavior
- Involve everyone
- Develop skills and potential
- Evaluate and measure continuously

STEP 1--PROVIDE A POSITIVE WORKING ENVIRONMENT

Motivation begins by first providing a positive work environment. Fran Tarkenton says, to find what motivates people, "you have to find what turns people on." This is the most important factor in the process. A motivating working environment requires going over and beyond the call of duty and providing for the needs of the worker.

Walt Disney World Company provides an excellent work environment for their employees or "cast members." Employee assistance centers are spread strategically across the theme park. Some of the services included employee discount programs, childcare information, money orders, postage stamps, check cashing, bus passes and 120 reward and recognition programs. The Walt Disney Company realizes that taking care of their employee's needs keeping them motivated, on the job and loyal to the company.

STEP 2—RECOGNIZE, REWARD, REINFORCE THE RIGHT BEHAVIOR

Mark Twain once said, "I can live for two months on a good compliment." Personal recognition is a powerful tool in building morale and motivation. A pat on the back, a personal note from a peer or a supervisor does wonders. Small, informal celebrations are many times more effective than a once a quarter or once a year formal event.

> *Recognition by one's peers is more powerful than traditional recognition by supervisors*.

Recognition by one's peers is more powerful than traditional recognition by supervisors. United Services Automobile Association (USAA) provides "Thank You" note stationary for their workers. Employees are encouraged to say "Thank You" to each other for the help they receive at work. The most surprising thing happened on the first day USAA printed the notes . . . they ran out! The company couldn't keep up with the demand.

STEP 3--INVOLVE EVERYONE

Having workers involved at all levels of the business is a key element improving morale and motivation. It also has a major impact on improving profit and productivity. The best way to involve workers is the use of teams and teamwork.

Businesses have found that teams improve productivity, increase morale and empower workers. Teams have decreased the need for excessive layers of middle managers and supervisors.

STEP 4--DEVELOP WORKER'S SKILLS AND POTENTIAL

Training and education motivates people and makes them more productive and innovative. At Federal Express, all customer contact people are given six weeks of training before they ever answer the first phone call. Learning never stops and testing continues throughout their employment tenure. Every six months customer service people are tested using an on-line computer system. Pass/fail results are sent to each employee within 24 hours. They receive a personalized "prescription" on areas that need reviewing with a list of resources and lessons that will help. Federal Express' intensive training and development program has resulted in higher motivation and lower turnover.

There are many reasons training and development makes sense. Well-trained employees are more capable and willing to assume more control over their jobs. They need less supervision, which frees management for other tasks. Employees are more capable to answer the questions of customers, which builds better customer loyalty. Employees, who understand the business, complain less, are more satisfied, and are more motivated. All this leads to better management-employee relationships.

STEP 5--EVALUATE AND MEASURE CONTINUOUSLY

Continuous evaluation and never ending improvement is the final step of the PRIDE system. Evaluation is a nonstop activity that includes a specific cycle of steps. The primary purpose of evaluation is to

> Businesses have found that teams improve productivity, increase morale and empower workers.

measure progress and determine what needs improving.

Continuous evaluation includes, but is not limited to, the measurement of attitudes, morale, and motivation of the workforce. It includes the identification of problem areas needing improvement and the design and implementation of an improvement plan.

Businesses have searched far and wide for the competitive advantage, the best equipment, robotics, or the latest business technique. It's about creating a work environment where people enjoy what they do, feel like they have a purpose, and feel they are reaching their potential. It requires more time, more skills and managers who care and are willing to try something different. It requires true leadership.

Gregory P. Smith

Chapter 1

Managing Team Ideas and Suggestions TNT

Ideas On-line: At BellSouth Mobility they put all their innovative ideas on an on-line computer program. "Quality Experts" (volunteers) work with the ideas if the persons submitting them cannot implement the ideas themselves.

Innovators Award: Create a monthly "Innovators Award" for those people who come up with a usable innovative idea. Allow workers time for innovation and capture their creativity with a contest for the best idea of the month.

Capture Ideas: Rubbermaid is a literal, innovative hotbed of ideas. They send their workers in search of new product ideas at off-the-wall places like museums, to study the Egyptians. The CEO, Mr. Wolf Schmitt, once visited a kitchen in China and discovered they used ordinary rubber spatulas to stir-fry food. Subsequently, he created a heat-resistant plastic spatula that could stand 500-degree heat. They are also working on a special bird feeder that uses a microchip to broadcast bird chirps into the owner's house. Every year they gather between 2,000 and 4,000 new ideas, then sift them down to the ones that can make money.

Anonymous Suggestion/Question Box: At Fortis Financial Group they use suggestion boxes for people to ask questions they don't feel comfortable asking in person. Management addresses the questions in a monthly newsletter.

> Do not ask for people's ideas unless you plan on implementing them.

Olinnovation: At the Olin Corporation they created a "future search team" that came together to create "Olinnovation." This team works within Olin to create an environment of innovation. They identify and train employees at all levels of the organization to be "idea scouts." A web page on Olin's intranet communicates and tracks the status of all ideas they generate.

Suggestion Exhibits: Use an adult "show and tell" program where employees bring their suggestions, ideas and new inventions for all to see. The organization provides a display area and time for this purpose. Although it is more readily used in a manufacturing or technically oriented company, the program has merit for service industries. It is a great way to increase networking and improve communication within any enterprise, and is more exciting and effective than suggestion boxes.

Suggestion Competitions: This more involved program was designed to encourage friendly competition between departments. Management asks departments to make suggestions. The number of suggestions per department are tabulated and posted each week (or month) on a wall chart in a public area. Special variations include an award for the best idea each week or month, and an award to the department having 100% participation. For even more fun, the department with the worst participation can also receive a special reward. This program is successful only if done with a spirit of enthusiasm and fun. Employee names should not be used. No fear or intimidation allowed.

Idea Olympics: The original form of Idea Olympics was an attempt to get people to think "out of the box." Toyota was one of the first companies to use this idea. The goal was to get people, while away from the office environment, to think creatively and innovatively about work. A group of people or a team meets away from the office, perhaps in a hotel or conference room. The group concentrates on new ways to reinvent the work process in a "no holds barred" think tank situation.

Good Idea Boards: The Buckhead (Georgia) Ritz-Carlton Hotel has a unique way to capture ideas and promote continuous improvement from their front line workers. Employees write their idea on an "easy wipe" board in their department. Instead of passing untested ideas up the chain of command, the employee who originates an idea has responsibility for its achievement. They follow a three-step work process: "study it, pilot it, and adopt it."

- A quality coach helps each department and its employees with the process. Once an idea is piloted and found worthwhile, they adopt it. Each month the department chooses the best idea. That idea is forwarded to the division, and then on to the Quality Office for special recognition.

- The department awards $10.00 for the best idea of the month. The best idea of the division gets $50 or brunch in the hotel's restaurant. At the

> A quality coach helps each department and its employees with the process. Once an idea is piloted and found worthwhile, they adopt it.

hotel level, the best idea receives $100 or dinner for two. In addition, the winners receive letters of appreciation and an invitation to a quarterly reception courtesy of the Ritz-Carlton Hotel.

- Ideas don't have to be big to be good. One innovative door attendant had the idea to pipe music into the first floor restroom. He talked to the engineering department director to see how hard it would be to implement. He and the engineering director went to the restroom, and found speakers and wires already in place. All they had to do was connect the wires, flip a switch, and the innovative idea came to life!

Idea Campaigns: Idea campaigns represent an upgraded and streamlined version of the old employee suggestion program, and are one of the best ways to get hundreds of ideas from your workforce in a very short time. Idea Campaigns provide one of the most significant and exciting ways of improving employee involvement.

Idea campaigns work hand in glove with all employee involvement programs. Use them to kick start customer service programs, improve performance, identify problems that cause errors, generate revenues and reduce expenses. The following organizations have done just that:

- Harley-Davidson saved $3,000,000 in one 30-day program.

- Holly Farms identified $1,000,000 in savings during a four-week program.

- Eaton Corporation gained 944 ideas from a workforce of 113 people, and had 100%

participation.

- Parker Hannifin Corporation received 499 ideas from 103 employees.

- National Semiconductor saved $3,600,000 using idea campaigns.

- The U.S. Park Service had over 12,000 employee suggestions with an approval rate of 75 percent.

Eglin Air Force Base in Florida ran a two-week idea campaign. The campaign asked all employees and military personnel to submit ideas that could reduce waste and inefficiency and increase productivity.

Eglin received a tremendous surprise when workers generated $400,000 worth of cost saving ideas and ways to generate new forms of revenue. The director of the program said the greatest reward was not the money saved, but the excitement and enthusiasm he now sees in his people. He said, "Now, once people have seen their ideas implemented, they are stopping me in the hallway to give me new ideas."

Wild, Crazy Idea Day: One day a month have employees bring in their craziest ideas on how to improve productivity. Each department creates some friendly competition about who can come up with the most, or the craziest, ideas as it affects productivity.

Top Guns: To get managers to more rapidly evaluate and decide on suggestions and ideas, Parker Bertea, a division of Parker Hannifin, created the Top Guns program. They selected two evaluators as "top guns," put their pictures on the bulletin board, and gave them "fighter ace" style hats to wear. The program reduced the average time for managers' decisions from six to two months.

Volunteer Noses: San Francisco saves the taxpayers money by using a cadre of volunteer "sniffers." When the public cries out about foul odors, the Public Works Department takes Odor Project volunteers to the suspected site in a specially equipped recreational vehicle. The volunteer sniffers use the city's special equipment to pinpoint the offending site, then call in officials for repair of treatment of the sewer system.

Reusable Coffee Mug Program: In an effort to educate the community about environmental issues, officials from Clifton, NJ made a reusable coffee mug. They figured that most people throw away 624 coffee cups a year, creating a massive burden on the environment. Their efforts focused on reducing the amount of disposable coffee cups and other forms of litter. The city gave these reusable mugs to merchants and "mom and pops" who sold coffee. The merchants agreed to sell the coffee at a discount to customers who returned with their mugs.

Not Invented Here: Raychem celebrates by stealing other department's ideas and applying them to a job. "Stealers" get certificates that say, "I stole somebody else's idea, and I'm using it." The person who had the original idea also gets an award. Their certificate says, "I had a great idea, and so-and-so is using it."

Amazon Books: Jeff Bezos founded the company, named after the longest river in the world. He moved to Seattle and hired his four employees. His first office was in his garage. Amazon now employs hundreds of people and literally is a virtual organization. They still do not have a storefront, but have access to over 2 million books. Many Amazonians' desks started off as unfinished doors sitting on sawhorses. Estimates say Bezos made $10 million in 1996. Forty-four percent of that was sales to repeat customers with estimated sales increases of 34% per month. Anyone who links their web site to Amazon can become part of the network and make 3-8% commission on each purchase someone makes through him or her. Amazon had 1800 associates sign up in a three-month period.

STAT VA: The Portland, OR Veterans Administration hospital has the STAT! (Slice Through Administrative Trivia) Idea Program. The STAT! Idea program encourages all employees to look for innovations or changes in work procedures that might save time and effort or reduce costs in their work area or service. Ideas can relate to any area under the purview of the hospital. Simplicity and fun are the hallmarks of this program. When an employee comes up with an idea, he or she first discusses it with the immediate supervisor. If the immediate supervisor agrees with the idea, it is then forwarded to the Service Chief. They send an idea form to the STAT! Idea Committee. It doesn't stop there. When the committee decides a STAT! Idea has wider application; they submit the idea to the Incentive Awards Suggestion program for an even greater cash reward. The award process is what holds this program together.

STAT Awards:

   Individual: Any STAT! Idea implemented generates an award for both the employee

> The Toro Company hired an independent inventor to come up with innovative ideas and improvements. He is exempt from going to meetings and the typical office functions that often detract from real work.

suggesting the idea and the immediate supervisor who approves the Idea. (This provides an incentive for the supervisor to approve the idea.) The first award is a choice of either a STAT! Coffee mug or a STAT! For the second and later ideas, both the employee and supervisor receive $10.00 for each implemented idea.

<u>Idea of the Month</u>: The STAT! Idea Committee reviews all ideas monthly and selects the "Idea of the Month." The Idea of the Month gets $50.00. Employees can submit unlimited ideas. Monthly winners are eligible for the "STAT! Idea of the Year" award.

<u>Annual Service Award</u>: The Committee selects the "Idea of the Year" winner with a $250 award to both the employee and supervisor. It also decides which department has the highest percentage of substantive implemented ideas per year. The winning department can receive up to $5000. Many departments have split the money and used it to have a department luncheon, buy new furniture, a refrigerator for the break area, and new computers for the staff.

Independent Inventor: The Toro Company hired an independent inventor to come up with innovative ideas and improvements. He is exempt from going to meetings and the typical office functions that often detract from real work. This way he is 100% available to his own creativity and ideas.

Employee Input: Ron Eardley, Executive Vice President of Image National, used employee input to help salvage the failing commercial sign designer and manufacturer. At off-site meetings he had all 77 employees review financial information, safety procedures and quality issues. He used employee-initiated teams to tackle problems and one project saved an estimated $40,000. Involving employees in the decision making process has also lowered turnover.

Idea Dollars: To spark team spirit and get more employee-generated ideas, use idea "dollars" printed on bright colored paper. During a specified time period (i.e., three months) whenever an employee generates an idea for team improvement or team projects they win one ticket. They cash in their tickets at the end of the game period for items such as team mugs, T-shirts, pencils, etc. Use team meetings to develop plans for using ideas you receive.

Intracapital and Intrapreneurs: Some corporations provide intracapital, a term used by Gifford Pinchot III in discussing intrapreneurs (basically, entrepreneurs within a large corporation). Ore-Ida selects five "fellows" every two years. Each one receives an annual budget of $50,000 to use in funding other employees in exploring new ideas.

The government might use this approach by creating a loan pool from which managers could borrow up to a certain limit. (Higher amounts would need executive or legislative approval.) The fund would put more control in the managers' hands, but make them responsible for repaying with money from their own budgets ventures that failed to generate a return.

Wild Hare Grants: Texas Instruments awards employees who have innovative ideas a "wild hare" grant for further research. They also give managers a degree of permission to award "IDEA grants" of up to $25,000 for prototype development.

This Smells: An issue of American Demographics had some interesting information about aromas and workplace productivity.

- Customers are more likely to shop, buy and return to stores that have a pleasant smell. Orange and spearmint worked the best; lavender and ginger were not as popular.

- A Japanese company found that keyboard operators improved their productivity when they used a lemon aroma. It also reduced stress levels.

- Peppermint and lavender help proofreaders catch more mistakes.

Gold Stars and Frogs: At Wachovia Bank, each Monday morning they set milestones for the week with input from staff members. On Friday, employees receive a Gold Star and $2.00 (funny money) for each milestone met. Employees can also recognize their peers with a sticker of a frog, which is worth $1.00. Staff members display the gold stars and frogs on a white cardboard poster. At the end of each month, they hold a random drawing for a dinner ($50.00) and movies ($25.00).

> At Wachovia Bank, each Monday morning they set milestones for the week with input from staff members.

Chapter 2

Energizing and Motivating Your Team TNT

Humor Corner: Give employees one corner of a break room or other area to post cartoons, illustrations and other items designed to relieve stress.   At the end of each week, the staff can award a prize for the best submission.

Star Charts: Help your employees become "stars." Post a wall chart with all departmental employees' names on it. Employees put gummed stars next to the names of people they feel deserve recognition for exemplary behavior. At month's end the person with the most stars gets a reward.

Crazy Hat Day: Create a special contest and have everyone wear the craziest hats to work.

Man Overboard Award: CIGNA believes in rewarding employees who go "over and beyond" for their customers. The "Man Overboard Award" is a life-saving ring, which the president presents to an employee at a special ceremony. CIGNA also pays teams for implemented ideas that improve productivity with awards as high as $25,000.

Consequences for the behavior you want is important

Flextime/flexshare: First Tennessee Bank believes that if you treat employees well they in return treat your customers well. The use of flextime and flexshare programs has resulted in double the loan volume handled since 1992 with no increase in staff or major changes in systems or technology. An additional bonus: a giant leap in customer service ratings.

Faux Paus Award: Sometimes it's fun to recognize an employee's goof. Try the "Faux Paus Award" - a plaque passed around the organization at a monthly social event with the current recipient's name engraved. The "keeper" of the award is responsible for selecting the next deserving recipient.

Fat Friday: Just about everybody loves to eat. At Texas A&M the first Friday of each month is celebration time. Everyone brings food to share, and they celebrate birthdays for that month as well as work anniversaries.

Free Lincoln Towncar: During the 80's, Truett Cathy, founder of Chick-Fil-A, wanted to increase sales by 40%. He offered to buy a new Lincoln Towncar for each facility manager who reached the goal, and gave away 47 cars in one year.

You Really Dazzle Me: The Gwinnett County Tax Commissioner's Office (Georgia) uses the department-wide "You Really Dazzle Me" program to recognize staff members who "go the extra mile" to help the department meet its vision statement, and to promote a positive work environment.

Employees are eligible for the award when they:

- Exceed customer expectations

- Provide superior quality work
- Demonstrate extraordinary, friendly, caring service
- Show a great deal of flexibility
- Demonstrate teamwork
- Go out of their way to solve a problem
- Reduce the cost of doing business
- Exhibit excellent recovery skills when correcting a problem to help a customer
- Show initiative

"You Really Dazzle Me" card winners are eligible for special awards each month through a random drawing while the person with the most cards automatically gets to choose a prize. Prizes include such things as mugs, cups, posters, paper holders, hats, etc., an extra 15-minute break, or an hour of comp time. Each "You Really Dazzle Me" winner also has his/her picture mounted on a special plaque placed at the employee's branch location.

Employee Dollars: At Phoenix Solutions Inc. employees award an "employee dollar" to fellow employees who do something special or exceed company expectations. Each month the employee with the most dollars gets movie tickets, dinner, and a plaque with their name as "Employee of the Month."

Lunch & Learn: Provide learning opportunities (movies, speakers, or classes) during lunch for workers who like to learn while they eat. Then recognize those who attend a certain number of events with an award or by putting their names in the company newsletter, or both.

Surprise Celebrations: Often it's the unexpected and informal that employees enjoy as much as formal awards. Conduct frequent, unannounced recognition and award celebrations, such as having a pizza party. If you don't know of a reason to have a get-together for the work force, invent one.

Dancing the Macarena: Employees at PeopleSoft, Inc. still haven't forgotten the day that CEO David Duffield danced the Macarena in front of 500 happy co-workers. Duffield doesn't act like a boss. His office is a cubicle; he answers his own phone and opens his own mail. Annual employee turnover is three percent, or one-quarter of the national average. Employees who earn outstanding service awards get either $500 in cash or 100 stock options.

Having Fun: Hal Rosenbluth, CEO of Rosenbluth International (the nation's fourth-largest travel services company) believes in creating a fun work environment. He starts by hiring "nice people," since he believes nice people like to work together and they like to have fun. Officers dedicate every Tuesday afternoon to serving high tea and discussing corporate values and other matters of importance to new recruits at the company's Philadelphia headquarters. There's a toll-free 800 number for any associate to contact Rosenbluth. He uses a sort of Crayola Rorschach test by sending associates crayons and blank paper to render their view of the company. A "happiness barometer" team meets every six months to benchmark attitudes and enjoyment levels.

Structured Spontaneity: Try some "structured spontaneity" like that practiced by Joel Slutzky, co-founder of Odetics Inc., a company that makes robots and spacecraft flight recorders. The company's chief technology officer appeared at the cafeteria cash register one St. Patrick's Day dressed as a leprechaun and dared anyone to outdo him! Managers also allow associates to cover the hallways with maps and photographs of their hometowns.

Car Detailing: Detailing is popular with today's car owners. Steve Cannon, a State Farm agent, hires a person to detail his employees' cars as a reward for special achievements.

After Dinner Phone Call: Even though you took time during the work day to thank the employee who went "above and beyond," go a step further and call them at home after dinner to say thanks. You'd be surprised how much this can mean to an employee. For teenage workers, call their parents and let them know you appreciate their son's or daughter's work.

Stress Handlers: Looking for a way to relieve employee stress? A credit card company has their employees write down the wildest reasons customers gave them for wanting more credit. Fellow employees vote for the craziest story, and give out prizes.

"Management by Fooling Around": Herb Kelleher, CEO and founder of Southwest Airlines, combines fun and hard work into something he calls "management by fooling around." At the nonconformist airline everything - from the tickets and boarding passes to the casual dress and occasional costumes attendants wear - clearly demonstrates that something is different.

One day each quarter all managers at Southwest work at a different job to help them learn more about the company. They may work as a luggage handler, gate agent, flight attendant, or some other position - as long as it is a front-line job.

Even Herb has helped load luggage onto the planes. Kelleher's wants his executives to be guiding examples. He also feels that everyone is a leader, and has attempted to limit rules and regulations so that people can make decisions at the lowest possible level. Kelleher says, "We tell our people that we value inconsistency."

There is a natural tendency for people and managers to become comfortable doing the same things the same way. Success lulls people to sleep. However, the innovative leader is always looking for ways to improve what is being done, never satisfied with just being good. In today's chaotic business environment, good is no longer good enough.

Be a risk taker-Leadership means you are in the front leading, not safely managing the rear of the formation. The innovative leader understands that progress depends on change and change is risky and scary. The leader creates an environment allowing people freedom to experiment and take risks without fear of reprisal. The innovative leader provides support and encouragement to his or her people even if a person fails in trying to do something new.

- Put managers and staff into the field to work with front-line workers several days each year.

- Reduce unnecessary regulations and policies. Paint a mailbox red and centrally place it so people can deposit all dumb rules and regulations needing revision or elimination. Form a team to evaluate each nomination. Celebrate with a bonfire burning all the policies and procedures no longer needed.

- If you haven't already, start a system of education and training program for everyone in the business.

- Practice true equality and eliminate all reserved parking spaces except for the disabled.

- Ask your workers frequently, "What can I do to make your job better, easier or more productive?" Then do it.

- Conduct frequent, unannounced recognition/award celebrations for workers.

- Give employees permission to disagree with management.

- Instead of only having the "Best Employee of the Month/Year" etc...Recognize individuals for different and positive reasons.

- Capture the creativity of people and have contests for the best idea of the month.

Breakfast with the President: The Human Resources Department of Nations Healthcare Inc. initiated a "Breakfast with the President" program to improve communications between employees and the CEO. Each breakfast begins at approximately 8:15 a.m., with coffee and biscuits served by the staff, and ends when the discussion ends. Results: higher morale and a sense of "openness."

Payday: The Milwaukee office manager for Manpower Inc. doesn't just give out paychecks on payday - employees also receive a Payday candy bar with their check.

The Candy Jar: I discovered the magical powers of a jar of candy on the desk when I worked in the Office of Innovation for the Army Medical Department. We tried to create a neutral zone where people could share their ideas, concerns, or just let off steam. People would come and first ask for a piece of candy, then start talking about frustrations, ideas, problems. Somehow that piece of candy seemed to serve as the catalyst for opening the lines of communication.

Oh, yes. Since our office had direct access to the commanding general's office we could take the ideas, problems and issues we heard directly to him. We were able to make many positive changes without a lot of unnecessary delays and paperwork.

Fun Fridays: A Dallas (Texas) unit of Sprint Corporation uses "Fun Fridays" to energize workers. Themes have included exchanging a plant with a co-worker, and ice cream socials where managers wore aprons and served sundaes.

Company Picnic: The cleaning products company, S. C. Johnson & Son Inc., (Racine, Wisconsin) hosted a picnic for 6000 company workers and their families.

Thrilling Thursdays: Employees of Nike Corp. (Beaverton, Oregon) can't wait for Thursday to roll around. They stop work at 4:30 in the afternoon and after some beer and soda they kayak across a lake, race bikes and compete in a 600-yard run.

Peat and Feet: Warehouse employees of Latana Peat & Soil, a subsidiary of Coventry Industries Corp. (Boca Raton, Florida) spend many hours on their feet as they move peat moss used on Christmas plants. Robert Hausman, chairman of

Coventry, rewards their long hours with a free visit to a podiatrist.

Bowling with Turkeys: Hotel tradition calls for employees at the Hyatt Regency (Lexington, Kentucky) to wrap a 12-pound frozen turkey with electrical tape, then roll it 50 feet down the loading dock (toward the human resource office!) and try to turn over as many wine bottle "bowling pins" as possible. Winners get a pumpkin pie.

The Stock Is Up!: Workers at the Chicago office of GATX Corp., a transportation services company, get a casual day whenever the stock hits a new high. The company even put a sign in the cafeteria which lists the closing price for the previous day so enthusiastic workers can keep tabs on company stock prices.

Post stock price for all to see

The World's Still Out There: The Atlanta office of A. W. "Bill" Dahlberg, Southern Co. CEO includes baseball caps, a nun puppet that can throw a punch, stuffed animals and gloves that make motorcycle sounds. Dahlberg keeps the items around to remind him there's a world outside his office with people who care what they're doing. The CEO believes in having fun, and has impersonated soul singer James Brown at company gatherings. He's also appeared dressed as Gen. George Patton, and once arrived decked out as a fortune teller complete with crystal ball.

Terrific Tuesday: When planning meetings or special projects, keep in mind that Monday seems to be the least productive day of the week. Tuesday is the most productive day before the mid-week slump begins on Wednesday and continues the rest of the week.

When was the last time you acted out a Three Stooges routine?

Keep it light: Meetings go better if you use rooms with lots of natural light, which tells the brain to produce serotonin. Serotonin makes people awake and alert, so stay away from meeting rooms with muted light.

Welcome "Cognoids": CEO Robert Shillman of Cognex, a Boston software company, welcomes new employees with a Three Stooges routine. Workers, known as "Cognoids," refer to Shillman as "Dr. Bob." The dozens of stunts he's dreamed up include leading them in a corporate anthem accompanied by an employee rock band, tossing moneybags with cash bonuses up to $10,000 out of a Brink's truck, and rewarding 15-year veterans with trips to one of the Seven Wonders of the World. Shillman believes his efforts help break down barriers between management and workers.

Souperman: Campbell Soup CEO David W. Johnson arrived in January, 1990 accompanied by trumpets sounding, "Mmmm, Mmmm, Good." The CEO once donned a red cape and called himself, "Souperman, Top Spoon," and on another occasion led a rally in a jockey's outfit. Johnson communicates his strategy and aligns his troops behind his vision, while backing his cheerleading with iron discipline.

"Enthusiastic Starts": At the beginning of each quarterly associates meeting at Professional Data, a software development company, practice something called enthusiastic starts. The president chooses 5 or 6 individuals from one department to present the enthusiastic start. The meetings usually start around 7:30 in the morning, so it's meant to be an "eye opener" and wake everyone up. Here are a few examples:

- They rewrote the YMCA song to fit the company. The group dressed up like the Village People and sang using hand motions and dance included. They also did a variation of "Brick House."
- They did a skit based on the television program, *Brady Bunch*, using computer software to portray the family in blocks as seen on the beginning of the show.
- Another skit based on Star Wars portrayed their competitors as the "dark side."

In addition to Enthusiastic Starts, Professional Data is working on a soft benefits plan. The idea is to increase time at home with family by having and outside service organization pick up and deliver employee's dry cleaning and take care of shoe repair and creating ease in getting cars detailed. Increase gym facility options; offer lawn services and garden maintenance, and an online service with the local grocery store.

Generate Competition! A tip from the US Air Force. Once each quarter the Wing Commander recognizes the airman, NCO and Sr. NCO of the quarter at a Commander's Call. Nominations come from within each unit, which then works to support their nominee, thereby generating competition between units.

Brown Bag Luncheon: An office at the Federal Energy Regulatory Commission uses brown bag luncheons as training initiatives.

Birthday Club: Energize your employees with fun! Once a month hold a Monthly Birthday Club celebration. At break-time, have special "goodies" and recognize employees who have a birthday that month with a card.

Reward Good Health: At Cornell University, an Excellent Attendance Program rewards employees who do not use a sick day within a six-months period with a day off, plus a certificate of recognition given at a special luncheon.

Improve Quality, Cost, Performance: At Melroe Company, employees who submit ideas to improve quality, cost, and performance are eligible for a $90.00 gift certificate to Wal-Mart. At a yearly banquet for all contributors, the company also gives larger cash awards and items such as televisions.

Butts for Balls: At Pine Oaks Golf Course, employees receive one bag of range balls for picking up one cup of cigarette butts.

A Work of Art at NASA: The graphics artist made caricatures of different groups and used the artwork pictures as awards which team members proudly display them on their desks. Eventually, everyone on the team got a picture.

Create an Employee Activity Fund: A tip from the Navy. Use an annual "auction" to raise employee activity funds. Management agrees to contribute (i.e., paying for a round of golf). Funds raised from the auction are used for office functions, etc.

A Day Without Meetings! Certain departments at the Atlanta Journal Constitution have "meeting free" Fridays.

Fun at Work: Consider these ideas to *boost employee morale.*

> **Work to Earn Time Off:** At Grayson College Golf Course, employees who did not miss a day of work for three weeks received a day off, which they could use on days when bad weather meant the course was not busy.

- At Certilman, Balin, Adler & Hyman (East Meadows, NY law firm) they hold a free lunch in the conference room each day for all 25 partners. Started as an opportunity to discuss business, it soon turned into an enthusiastic social gathering.

- At JW Genesis Financial Corp. (Boca Raton, FL), Vice-Chairman Joel Marks allows workers to view TV-sitcom tapes (such as "Seinfeld") during the lunch break.

- Southwest Airlines encourages crewmembers to joke with the passengers.
- Terry Deal, business professor at Vanderbilt University, Nashville, TN, has noted that companies, which allow some play in the workplace often, realize higher profits.

Meditation Rooms for Employees: Job-related stress is an undeniable part of today's world. According to estimates of the National Safety Council, one million employees are absent on any workday due to stress-related issues. To cope with this, some companies offer "meditation rooms." At Acacia Life Insurance Co. (Bethesda, MD-based) and PT & Co. (NYC), rooms with dim lights, comfortable chairs and couches and without telephones provide a place for employees to "get away from it all" for a few minutes. This time of respite enables the employees to return to their work areas refreshed.

Consider using "Safety Jackpot" to improve your company's safety record: According to Peavey Performance Systems (Lenexa, KS) hundreds of companies including Amoco Oil, Coca-Cola, Kellogg's, General Electric, Miller Brewing and Kraft Foods have used their Safety Jackpot Program to improve safety performance and reduce accidents.

The program uses scratch-off game cards as an incentive for safety. Accident-free employees, who meet certain safety criteria, receive a game card (worth 25, 50, 75 or 100 points) each week. Award game cards for individual achievement, team achievement or both. Employees then redeem their points/game cards for brand-name merchandise from the Safety Jackpot catalog.

Each game card also has one letter found in J-A-C-K-P-O-T. Employees whose accumulated cards spell "jackpot" receive a thousand bonus points and become eligible for a grand-prize drawing.

For more information about the program, contact: Peavey Performance Systems, 14865 W. 105th Street, Lenexa, KS, 66215; (800) 235-2495; fax (913) 888-3898.

Chapter 3

Removing Barriers and Creative Problem-Solving TNT

Issue Board: An "issue board" at S. C. Johnson Wax encourages every employee to participate in problem solving. The team leader or department head tapes a piece of flip-chart paper on a wall and writes the problem/issue at the top of the sheet. During the week employees write their solutions/comments on the paper and may also list similar issues that stem from the main one. After about a week they remove the "issue board" and use the staff's ideas to remedy the issue or solve the problem. This method lets the group understand that management considers the problem important and in need of attention, and also helps to focus the group's energy on the problem. It also encourages participation by those who don't speak up in staff meetings.

One Step Further: Carry the idea a step further and allow the person who offered a marketable, innovative idea to form a team to develop it.

Solution Central: In-house bureaucracy a problem? At one time, IBM initiated a "Solution Central" special service desk. The sole purpose of the desk, which has 50 people on call 95 hours a week (including weekends) is to help employees overcome bureaucracy.

Internal Defect Form (IDF): **Doing** it right the first time is more than just a philosophical statement. According to Mr. Hortz Shulzte, CEO of Ritz-Carlton, they increased sales while using less man-hours by eliminating defects, rework and unnecessary steps in their key processes.

Employees who notice a deficiency or defect complete an IDF. All IDFs are collected and forwarded to the hotel's Quality Office for consolidation, then sent to the appropriate department for action. Department managers and Quality Coaches then take the necessary action to repair, replace, or advise the staff of the problem. The hotel's goal is to eliminate all defects. In 1995, only 6.4 percent of customers experienced a defect during their stay as compared to 30 percent in 1992.

> All IDFs are collected and forwarded to the hotel's Quality Office for consolidation, then sent to the appropriate department for action.

"Proceed Until Apprehended:" There's more than one-way to work within a bureaucracy as one Mayor of Los Angeles, discovered. When he wanted to remove an unneeded tow-a-way zone on a public street in the garment district he had to challenge a 25-page memorandum full of rules and regulations requiring various permissions, hearings, and other hurdles to clear. The Mayor's impatience and frustration with the system apparently prompted others to action. One night an official and his son simply removed all the signs. Apparently, "If you can't work with the system go around it."

Business Credit Cards: Try providing your employees with business credit cards to purchase office supply items, repair parts, etc. Place some reasonable restrictions on how much they can charge without prior approval and use the system to save time for everyone when employees need basic supplies quickly. It can also help relieve the feeling that they're overwhelmed with paperwork for even the simple things.

B.S. Stamp: Give employees the chance to point out unnecessary paperwork with the use of special "B.S." rubber stamps on redundant or unnecessary paperwork or documentation. All paperwork with the stamp goes to a designated individual for evaluation, and, if appropriate, termination.

Red Mailbox: Another version of the "get rid of the unnecessary" paperwork theme: paint a mailbox red and place it in a central location. People can deposit in the mailbox all the items they consider dumb, including non-value-added rules and regulations. Create a special team to evaluate the "deposits" and either revise or eliminate them. Use a giant bonfire to burn the eliminated "dumb" policies and procedures.

Limit Those Signatures: If you're requiring more than two signatures/approval levels on correspondence, take time consider whether you really need all those signatures. Eliminating unnecessary multiple signatures can save time and hassle for everyone involved.

"Ceremonial Funerals:" Getting rid of old policies, outdated rules, regulations, systems, that get in the way of progress. Focus on the transformation to the new way of doing things by having a "funeral" to bury or burn bureaucratic red-tape.

Wainwright Industries introduced a series of changes to create a "barrier free" environment

> **Postage "Honor" System:** Many employees today bring their personal mail to the office for postal pick-up. Use an "honor" system that allows individuals to buy stamps for personal mail. Employees will appreciate the convenience, and it also helps to remove the temptation for them to use business postage for personal mail.

where everyone feels they are part of a team. The company calls workers "associates," eliminated all reserved parking spaces (except for handicapped), replaced office walls with glass (including the CEO's office), has everyone including management wear a uniform, abolished time clocks and put everyone on salary, allows workers to evaluate managers and developed a profit-sharing program for everyone. Trust between the associates and management has taken a giant leap forward.

The increased feeling of trust, equality and ownership has produced excellent results. Since 1984, with the exception of one year, attendance has consistently averaged 99 percent. Profits have grown from $5 million to $30 million. Obviously, this company is doing something right.

Wainwright and Rewarding Mistakes: Many people like to talk about trust and equality, but Wainwright Industries understands that if you want people to learn, if you want innovative ideas, if you want people to fix problems - then you can't punish them for accidents. (They believe that most accidents are not people problems, but system problems.)

Wainwright tackled this problem at a plant in Texas where they were trying to instill the new culture of trust and equality. When workers accidentally damaged doors with their equipment, they didn't report the accidents due to fear of dismissal.

This changed when an employee took a chance and admitted his accident to Don Wainwright. CEO Wainwright called a plant-wide meeting, explained to everyone what had happened, then called the man up and shook his hand in front of everyone! Overnight people started reporting accidents. With the elimination of fear of punishment accident reporting went from zero to 90 percent. Now they can openly identify, then fix or repair, defects and other accidents that eat at the bottom line.

Wainwright's Continuous Improvement Process (CIP): In 1994 associates *Implemented* over 8,400 improvement ideas. They presently average 300 ideas a week from 146 associates. The associates - not management - totally run this powerful process. This works because associates at Wainwright have authority to make changes up to $1000 in cost. If their idea or change exceeds this amount, they fill out an AFE (Authorization for Expenditure) form to get administrative approval. Each week they have random drawings for prizes. Two people win $50 cash each for safety CIPs (Continuous Improvement Process) and two people win $50 cash each for regular CIPs. The previous week's winner makes the drawings. The company also has quarterly drawings for a $300 gift certificate, and it comes with a catered luncheon for everyone who submitted a CIP during that quarter.

Ask Your Workers: Managers should frequently ask their workers, "What can I do to make your job better, easier or more productive?" Then listen!

Theybusters: Roger Sant, CEO of AES felt that many people in the company perceived there was someone - "They" - above them preventing them from doing the right thing. He created a special campaign called "Theybusters" designed to eliminate bureaucratic work habits and thinking. He kicked off the "Theybusters" campaign with buttons and posters displaying the word "They" with a red line through it.

Gold Badges: Top management at Sharp decides which projects are the most important. Team members for these projects wear gold badges and everyone in the company knows this means their request must be dealt with immediately.

"But Sir...": A new commanding officer who reports aboard his/her ship hands out a special poker chip with the words, "But Sir...." This encourages lower ranking personnel to question directions and make suggestions. It also helps set the values and vision of the new C.O.

Take-a-Risk Coupons: Try distributing to workers a printed "coupon" that they can redeem for one "Risk Taking Opportunity."   If someone tries something new and fails, they can redeem the coupon to their manager/supervisor. Management must accept the coupon with no repercussions.

Take-a-Risk Poker Chips: This is a variation of the "Take-a-Risk Coupon."   In lieu of coupons, issue poker chips to workers. When the time comes, the worker can cash in his/her poker chip.

Stolen Ideas: "I had a great idea, and so-and-so is using it."   This idea comes from Raychem (HBR) where employees celebrate when they steal another department's ideas and apply them to a job. The employee who "stole" the idea receives a certificate: "I stole somebody else's idea, and I'm using it." The person who had the original idea also receives a certificate: "I had a great idea, and so-and-so is using it."

Logo Contest: At Cornell University, one section held a logo contest as a way to unite the people and the departments in that area.   Everyone who submitted an idea received a prize.

Be a Giraffe: At GSA, they gift Giraffe Awards to people who "stick their neck out" and take risks-- even if unsuccessful.

True Leader: At the Office of Naval Intelligence, the Chief of Staff (Captain in the Navy) spends half-a-day with each sailor, regardless of rank or rating, as a way to become familiar with the sailors' jobs. Sailors view the practice as both supportive and encouraging.

A New Use of Yellow Stickies: At Experian, a post-it board in the workroom features an idea subject or problem, written at the top of the board, each month. Employees write ideas to solve the problem on the yellow sticky (with their name written on back of post-it). The person with the most imaginative solution receives a prize, and there is also an additional random drawing for prizes.

Suggestion Boxes that Work: At Bic Corp. (based at Milford, CT), employee-involvement made the difference in the effective use of the employee suggestion box. Hourly workers run the program, which calls for prompt removal of suggestions from the box and a response (guaranteed) within ten days. Employees with winning suggestions earn "Bic Bucks" which they can redeem at the company cafeteria or exchange for cash. The result: savings for the company; boosted employee morale.

Find Out About Employee Satisfaction: Some recent studies have linked employee-satisfaction at work with customer-satisfaction. Sun Computer Company polls workers through e-mail questionnaires in an effort to discover "performance inhibitors"-- situations which employees feel interfere with their performance at work. Discovered problems include "excessive workload" and lack of "people resources."

Look Out for the SWAT Team: Mervyn's (department store chain, 270 locations in 14 states, 32,000 employees) created its own SWAT team to handle company crises. Team members (managers with expertise in either buying, merchandising, or advertising) go wherever needed in the company's buying divisions. The team, which started several years ago as an experiment in dealing with workforce issues, today helps the company handle a variety of issues, including staffing needs and erratic markets. Highly trained team members can do the work quickly and efficiently without the learning time that would otherwise be required. Young people with a desire to move up in the company and veteran employees looking for a change of pace view joining the SWAT team as a high-priority career move.

Reinventing the Government: Government employees have received "Reinventing Government Team Member" cards to help them stay focused on their goals. It reads:

We will invent a government that puts people first, by -
- Putting Customers First
- Cutting Red Tape
- Empowering Employees To Get Results
- Cutting Back To Basics

[signed]

Bill Clinton   Al Gore

The other side of the card reads:

Here's how: We will -
- Create a clear sense of mission
- Steer more, row less
- Delegate authority and responsibility
- Help communities solve their own problems
- Replace regulations with incentives
- Develop budgets based on outcomes
- Inject competition into everything we do
- Search for market, not administrative, solutions
- Measure our successes by customer satisfaction

Chapter 4

Finding, Attracting & Hiring Team Members TNT

Quench Your Search: TRC Staffing, a temporary help agency in Conyers, GA, found a new way to tell people about their service. They pass out small bi-fold cards with packets of drink mix glued inside. Printed on the outside of the card: "Quench your search for temporary help by calling TRC Staffing Services Today!!!"

The Underemployed: Ron Self, senior vice president of metro markets for Norrell Corp., an Atlanta-based temporary help firm, decided to focus on the underemployed, those working less hours than they would like, and the intellectually underused, to remain competitive in the too-small available labor pool.

Internet: Pat Vogeler, human resources director for Alcatel Network Systems (Raleigh, North Carolina) turned to the Internet to fill vacancies and gets about 25 percent of the new hires today from a job-searching Web site.

Recruiters and Professors: Kim Sharpton, Enterprise Rent-a-Car's north Alabama human resources manager, came up with a new recruiting idea. In addition to on-campus student recruiting sessions, they conduct invitation-only get togethers for the professors and urge them to encourage students to consider Enterprise's management training program.

Imported Workers: Human resource managers at Gaylord Entertainment Co.'s Opryland Hotel, a Nashville-area facility, imported and housed workers from Puerto Rico to fill staffing needs. They also hired school bus drivers for summer duty and provided free transportation for workers as far away as 50 miles. The company also sent a personnel team to Jersey City, New Jersey to recruit newly arrived Egyptian immigrants and hired 300 for jobs from housekeeping to staff retail shops. Gaylord also had Opryland provide subsidized housing on company property to help the immigrants get started. Hotel staff members helped them set up checking and savings accounts so they can prepare to rent on their own.

Association Joiner: Kristine Gibson, founder of Isotech (a recruiting firm in Morrisville, NC) is a member of ten different associations and spends about 10 hours a week attending committee meetings. Her firm specializes in recruiting for technology firms and her recruiting successes through these contacts more than repay her membership expenses.

Tacit and Explicit: The Japanese rely on tacit knowledge, that which comes from your personal experience and what you feel when you have a hunch. It's not purely rational, but connected to your emotions and beliefs. Americans depend on explicit knowledge: information we can verbalize, write down in documents, put into our computers and communicate. To create knowledge, we need a convergence of tacit and explicit knowledge.

Human resources: View people as strategic resources. In Japan some of the best employees go into human resources. Some employees have a richer knowledge base than others and understanding this is important if you are forced to have lay-offs.

Shopping for Workers: Frank E. Evans, chief executive of EFS Inc. (a Montgomery-based firm that owns and operates pawn shops throughout Alabama and in Charlotte, NC) sends his managers to the malls to shop for clerks. They recruit people from retailers they think are doing a particularly good job of serving the public. The plan offers employees cash bonuses of $50 to $250 for every new hire.

Teachers for Industry Program: Mike Waldrip, materials manager at Veratec (nonwoven fabrics manufacturer, Athens, Georgia) worked with the local Chamber of Commerce and school system to form the Teachers for Industry Program. Teachers of high school and junior high school students visit the local factories during the weeklong program in the summer. The goal is to show the teachers the opportunities that manufacturing today offers to students who aren't headed for college.

Creative Employee Benefits: The Los Angeles Department of Power and Water (LADPW) offers its 11,000 employees such benefits as a free seven-week lunch time series on nutrition, prenatal care, use of health benefits; an ob-gyn/pediatric nurse comes two days a week to answer medical questions; electric nursing pumps for mothers to provide milk to babies at child care (and dads can take the devices home to their partners); certified social workers to help employees use programs and resources; parenting classes at lunch time; support groups for parents. It also offers four-month maternity and paternity leaves, a resource center for parents, and a beeper that lets expectant fathers know when their wives go into labor. After the agency discovered that the cost of employee absence due to caring for children ran around one million dollars a year, it subsidized a childcare center for employees. The center generates its own revenues.

Employee-friendly Company: Phyliss Brody and Evelyn Greenwald, co-owners of Creativity for Kids (Cleveland, Ohio) allow some workers to work four-day weeks and take unpaid leave in summer when children are home. In this employee-friendly company workers say "we" and "our" when speaking about the company and feel free to go to Phyliss and Evelyn with their problems. The owners tell employees when they've done a good job, are willing to hire workers' family members, and provide extra leave to employees with sick children or family members. They even help second shift workers pay for taxis home. Walls painted sunshine yellow with photos of employees' children posted everywhere emphasize the friendly working environment.

Lunch as a Family: Freddie Mac, a mortgage concern in McLean, Virginia, added baby highchairs and booster seats so that workers could have their babies and young children with them at lunch time.

Employee Equity: Nashville-based First American Corp. designed incentive packages (stock) to encourage seasoned employees in key positions to stay with the company, thereby reducing the cost of turnover in strategic positions.

Unusual Benefits: Wilton Connor of Wilton Connor Packaging (Charlotte, North Carolina) offers employees some unusual benefits at a modest cost: two laundresses each shift who wash, dry and fold employees' family laundry while they work; a handyman who makes repairs at workers' houses; and vans to transport workers to and from work including stops at day-care centers.

Use imaginative recruiting in a tight job market. If you find it hard to recruit workers, despite increased pay and benefits, consider these innovative approaches.

- Telesec CoreStaff (Kensington, MD temp firm) set up a recruiting table at a Frederick, MD minor-league baseball game.

- The Protestant Guild (Waltham, MA), a learning center for mentally disabled children, advertised for on the back of grocery receipts for teachers and other help.

- Theme parks and fast-food firms in the Long Beach, CA area use banners pulled behind airplanes to recruit workers.

- Recruit good employees...from other businesses. More than one company has started sending its managers on "stealth" missions. They go around the mall "shopping" for good clerks. When they encounter someone they believe would make a good employee for them, they invite them to apply. In a slightly different setting, a worker in a snack bar at a golf course received approximately ten job offers from golfers.

Chapter 5

Customer Service TNT

Here's Looking at You: Tone of voice accounts for 38 percent of any given communication. A mirror placed in front of customer service representatives who handle telephone calls helps the employees visualize their attitudes and expressions. The employees transfer this attitude to the customer through their tone of voice. A positive attitude shows, even over the phone.

Adding Value: Journey's, (27 stores, part of Genesco, Inc., Nashville, TN), increased shoe sales 26 percent in 1996 when they focused on teenage customers by providing music videos. They also used an even bigger "bait" - telephones located inside the stores. The phones (some free, some pay phones) add value as well as attract those teenagers who "hang out." (In case things get out of hand, the phones do have cut-off switches.)

The Lost Sock: The Lost Sock, a laundromat in Richmond, VA, has added a total new dimension to the soapy floors and broken washers normally found in most laundromats. Every Thursday night they have an "open mike" event. About 100 guests come to wash their laundry, have a few beers and watch their friends perform.

Customer Lists: Have each person and/or department make a list of their customers. Then have a contest for ideas on the most spectacular way to serve those customers. Publicly display the customer list and what each employee did for their customer(s).

Focus on Patients: Griffin Hospital in Derby, CT, faced with stiff competition and higher patient expectations, developed patient-focused programs that have become a model for other health care systems. The changes were not easy, but resulted in a remarkable transformation.

The hospital began by enhancing the patients' surroundings with water fountains, fish tanks, green plants, and terraces. A piano on each floor and strolling violinist provides music for relaxation and enjoyment. The changes also include a focus on art with a display of work by local artists and programs such as puppets and a dance program.

Other changes included:

Visiting Hours: There are no age restrictions for visitors, and in fact people can visit or even stay overnight if the patient approves.

Open Doors: The library is open to everyone, not just the staff.

Medical Information: The hospital provides patients with fact sheets about their individual medical problems. They also post medical records on a wall outside the room so family members and the patient can see them.

Food: Patients have more control over what they eat. Don't like the hospital meal? Then order a sandwich from the deli! A volunteer will deliver it to your room. Each ward has a kitchen where patients or family members can cook a meal. Volunteers come to bake fresh cookies; jello and ice cream are available 24 hours a day.

ICU: The Intensive Care Unit is shaped like a wagon wheel with pods on the outer edges. The area has family rooms outside the circle and no restrictions on visitation. Carpeting throughout the unit provides a quiet environment. They also eliminated the electrical noise found in many units. Fish tanks are part of the furnishings in ICU, and quiet background music provides a pleasant atmosphere. The nurses do everything, and patients receive 70 percent of their treatment and care in the room - no more shuttling patients back and forth.

Volunteer Handholding Program: Volunteers are available to hold the hands of patients who come in for same-day surgery. This soft-touch program reduces stress and the aloneness many patients experience. For example, a volunteer may sit with an eye surgery patient. If the patient has to move or sneeze, they squeeze the volunteer's hand so as not to disrupt the surgery. As a result, the patient is less anxious, quieter and doesn't move around as much.

Staff Retreats: The patients aren't the only ones benefiting from the changes at Griffin Hospital. Griffin wants everyone, from the custodian to the surgeon, to consider themselves care givers. Each month the hospital holds a two-day retreat at which approximately 20 staff members experience what

> The power of touch has a calming impact on people during stress.

it's like to be a patient and depend on someone else for care. They share a room with someone they don't know, have no choice about their food, must feed each other and lead one another blindfolded. The idea is to help staff members think about how the patient feels when someone else must do things for them, and to understand how it feels to lose control over one's life. The goal is for all staff members go through the retreat experience.

Customer Driven Company - Company management had all employees complete a survey (from a book of the same name). After they tabulated the results, they used the information during meetings to discuss ways the company could improve.

Guest Service Fanatic - Employees like to get "carded" at Disney's Contemporary Resort in Florida. Staff members who provide excellent service to guests receive a pre-printed "card." All the cards go in a box, and each month the resort holds drawings during "Guest Service Fanatic" celebrations.

Focus Groups - Try allowing front-line service personnel to form focus groups and survey needs and wants of customers.

Downtown Dollars - Looking for a way to encourage shoppers to support downtown merchants? Then consider what the local merchants association and retailers in State College, PA accomplished. To keep people shopping downtown instead of going to the competing malls they developed a unique gift certificate program, which uses special gold (brass) coins. Each coin is worth one dollar and has the inscription, "Downtown Dollar Gift Certificate." People use the coins in place of cash. Not only did the program result in more shoppers downtown supporting local merchants, but also the coins have become a collectors item used as gifts and fuel for incentive programs.

A Hot $2 Bill: Looking for something to give your customers that will stay with them for a while? Consider this idea from Chile Chompers. The shop, located in Stone Mountain, GA, specializes only in hot sauces and spices. They include a $2.00 bill with a little red pepper-shaped sticker on it in each customer's change. The sticker has their store name and phone number. Since most people don't give out $2 bills, customers usually carry them in their wallets for a long time.

When Little is Big: Robert Kenimer, a State Farm Insurance agent in Carrollton, Georgia, uses business cards that are a third smaller in size than normal. In small red print at the bottom of the card: "If I could get your business, I could afford a bigger card." On the back: "832-2468, Who do we appreciate?"

Tiffany's "T-Clips": Tiffany, based in New York, publishes the "T-Clips" newsletter, which is devoted to stories about exceptional customer service and identifies employees in all areas who were part of an extra effort. They recognize that success requires teamwork and sales support staff and others share the credit when sales representatives make monthly goals.

Making Money by Having Fun: At the three Jordan's Furniture three stores in New England, owners Barry and Eliot Tatelman use unusual tactics to keep the customers entertained and coming back. They have animated figures and a remote-controlled character on a tricycle, wash customers' car windows, pass out umbrellas on rainy days, and sometimes offer complimentary treats (popcorn, cookies, ice cream). The owners also installed a $2.5 million simulation theater at one store.

They consider the customer's perspective when setting up displays and groupings, use background music and scents for theme areas, welcome customers with maps of the store, have clear signage throughout the store and provide clearly marked restrooms with baby changing areas. The owners monitor product quality with computerized quality problems by vendor and type of problem and pay attention to reports from repair technicians. They teach sales associates to focus on product knowledge rather than just closing the sale. "Sleep technicians" in white lab coats work in the bedding department. They see a customer with a problem as an opportunity to make a fan.

No One's Done That: Just because someone else hasn't done it doesn't mean you can't. California Casket Co. had a display at the Los Angeles County Fair to show their coffins, urns and grave markers. President Rob Karlin thought it would be a good idea, and items included a denim covered coffin and an urn shaped like a cowboy boot.

It Pays to Read: Norwood Davis, CEO of Trigon Blue Cross/Blue Shield in Virginia, was so impressed with the customer service book, "A Complaint is a Gift," (Janelle Barlow and Claus Moller) that he offered employees $100 each for reading the book. The offer required employees to note five ideas they got from the book and suggest three ideas they could use.

Taste This: Ben & Jerry's Ice Cream sponsor ice cream tasting contests for both internal and external customers. They give away candy and other prizes for people who have helped taste and develop new ice cream flavors.

Getting to Know the Customer: One company runs quite a few off-shore business meetings every year for their customers. Every employee in the company gets to go on at least one of these trips. (And they go to some really exotic locales.) They can take a spouse or significant other too and the company picks up the tab. It allows the employee to meet customers of the company, people who they never see but speak with on the phone or correspond with via E-mail. At the meeting they establish a face-to-face relationship with the customer and get to know each other on a personal basis. In most cases, the employee picks up valuable info about the customer that the company can then use to gain additional business or make changes in the way they serve that customer. And end up getting more business by making the changes. It fosters the "partnership" aspects of the business, both internal and external.

Donated by Phil Steffen, CSP, CPAE. The Bottom Line Group

Competition

Businesses can no longer compete strictly on price of goods and services alone. The next decade will be a battleground with few winners. It will be a time of intense competition and the winners will be the ones who know exactly what they are doing.

The primary competitive advantage of the 90's and beyond is how and the speed in which you meet your customers needs. The recipe for exceptional customer service boils down to a few basic

> **Be Visible:** Manage by walking around and observing. A management visible to the work force can be very valuable. --US Air Force

ingredients. Some of those ingredients are flexibility, friendliness, speed, and exceeding customer needs and expectations. . .lots of little things that make tremendous differences.

Blue Willow Inn is one hour west of Atlanta in Social Circle, Georgia. Friends decided to eat at this antebellum restaurant that they had heard so much about. Food was on the table when they overheard Vivian, the waitress, tell guests at another table that they didn't accept credit cards. My friends panicked when they realized that they might not have enough cash to pay for their meal. They asked Vivian if what they heard was true.

She confirmed the fact; no, they didn't accept credit cards; but Vivian quickly countered with this statement. "Don't let that ruin your meal. You see I have my own money and I will pay for your meal." She opened her purse and she showed them her cash. My friends were in shock and couldn't believe what they just heard. The waitress was going to pay for their meal! They will never forget Vivian or the Blue Willow Inn.

If you are going to survive as a customer business, you are going to have to provide unequaled customer service, no exceptions. Right or wrong, the customer is always right. The result will be greater satisfaction for both workers and customers and an exceptional bottom line. Here are some key points to keep in mind.

• Build a long-term relationship with your customers, not a one-night stand. Call your customers on the phone or stand at the door as they are leaving. Ask them how they were treated, what you could have done better. Will they return to buy something else?

• Pretend you are the customer and evaluate your own business. Use a telephone and call your business up. How long does it take to get an answer? How are you handled? Do they use your first name? Did they make you feel welcome or were you treated like a nuisance?

• Measure what's important to your customers. The customer, not management, decides what exceptional service is. Identify what they need and expect and develop a system to show how well you are doing in each area that is important to your customers.

• Use the Internet. Can you provide sales, service or information on the internet? More and more people are using the web for everything from fine wines to contact lenses.

• Handle all customer complaints with enthusiasm. For every one complaint there are at least 10 other customers that visited your business who have the same complaint. A portion of the 10 just took their business to your competitor. If you solve the problem, you will have a more loyal customer.

• Build loyal employees. The front-line person is the most important person in your organization. Treat them like the way you treat your customers. We all know how difficult it is to find and keep good workers. If they feel management cares about them, they will reflect the same respect to your customers.

Use "hero awards." Make heroes out of your customer service people and allow coworkers to reward each other for doing a good job.

- Provide a customer service guarantee that excites people. Customers are sick of loopholes and limited warranties. People are tired of hassles and long lines and forms to fill out. Sure, there will be people who will take advantage of you, but the trade-off is a lot more people who will buy, visit, tell their friends about and spend their money on you and not on your competitor.

- Don't stop; continuously improve all areas relating to customer service. The competition never stops, neither should you. Evaluate and visit other good businesses and see what they are doing.

Chapter 6

Improving Communication and Meetings TNT

Summit Quest: Jostens designed this video communication plan featuring the company's four major objectives. Each video addresses one objective, is approximately 10 minutes long, and is done in a professional and energetic manner. The videos help the work force understand the company's goals and objectives improving communication from the top-down.

Audio Tape: The National Speakers Association uses a monthly audiotape to communicate to its 4000-plus members. (NSA recognized the fact that many people spend a great deal of time in their automobiles where they could listen to the tape.) The audiotape provides all types of information including interviews with speakers, health and fitness techniques, information on upcoming events, and news important to the speaking professional.

Organizational Rolodex: Abbott Laboratories provides each employee with Rolodex cards identifying all members and their area(s) of expertise. This provides a record, or database, of each person's training, skills and experiences.

Employees can draw upon the information to help implement ideas and form teams. The "Rolodex" is also available on the e-mail system.

Ten-Minute Meetings: Some Japanese companies practice "Chorei" staff meetings each morning. These ten-minute meetings at which employees stand up - no chairs allowed - provide a strong beginning for the day. It worked for Caterpillar and Mitsubishi when they jointly developed a hydraulic shovel.

Hallway Training: A study to see how much information co-workers shared informally demonstrated that during a typical week at one company over 70 percent of the 1000 workers in the study shared information with fellow employees. Fifty-five percent asked co-workers for advice. It all happened during meetings; exchanges with customers, supervisors and mentors; on-the-job training; site visits; cross training; shift changes; same-level employee communication; and **simply by doing one's job.** The next time you see employees talking during shift changes, in the halls, or at coffee breaks, remember that you may be witnessing learning in progress.

French Fry Rally: In a memo to owners and operators of McDonald's restaurants in the US, vice-chairman Jack M. Greenberg called upon them to rally together to neutralize a competitor's assault upon their famous French Fries. First he reminded them that "...McDonald's has the best fries...." Then he called upon everyone to work together as a team to "...affirm our fries superiority on the frontline." He gave three basic and specific guidelines for all operations to follow. He also reminded them that, "Nobody can beat us when we do it right." In other words: tell your people the problem, tell them why and how you can win, and then remind them how good they are.

Blank Agenda: For a more productive staff meeting with more staff participation post a blank meeting agenda in the employee area. Employees jot down questions and/or issues for staff meetings. You'll also discover many practical topics and concerns you weren't aware of previously.

"I Want To Be Alone": Unlike former screen star Greta Garbo; you don't have to retire and go into seclusion if you want to be left alone. Employees at City-Search, a travel firm based in North Carolina, wear a red sash to signal to others that they're not available for conversation. The idea is to help the workers stay focused. An e-mail message advises workers who want to try the idea that they can borrow a sash from the coat rack. Chatty co-workers know to leave fellow employees alone when they "see red."

Cooking Right Along: United for a Fair Economy, a labor group based in Boston, has produced a 100-page book for unions to use as a guide on staging creative outdoor rallies and "media stunts." It's called, *The Activity Cookbook: Creative Actions for a Fair Economy.*

Stuff the Staff Meeting: Bob Felton, a former Navy Commander and now President of Indus Group (software developer with 400 employees), believes that most staff meetings become a time-wasting venture so he eliminated all routine staff meetings. It is okay to hold meetings when they are really needed. He follows two rules: 1) Delight your internal and external customers; and 2) Use your best judgment.

> **Gasshuku:** The Japanese have "gasshuku" or off-site meetings or camp-ins where the barriers come down when team members camp in hotel and exchange ideas.

Skip-Level Meetings: Hold skip level, idea meetings with both hourly and salary employees. By mixing hourly and salary workforce with management helps create a pleasing mix of ideas. Providing either pizza or donuts always makes it a better meeting.

Share the News: The Bethany Care Society share staff member's successes & ideas through a bimonthly newsletter, which they attach to the pay stubs of every employee.

The Union Wins: Union Leadership-Union leaders with the Hawaii State Teachers Association give recognition to members of management who are outstanding leaders. This improves communication and trust between union and management.

Hair-on-Fire: Put your to-do list on a white board next to your desk. So when your boss or a manager comes in with an urgent "hair-on-fire" project, ask the person which of the other projects should you put on hold? I attach the name of the manager/customer next to the project-so the "urgent" manager can see whose project(s) they are stopping or slowing. Then ask them to mention their "jumping ahead in line" to the manager whose project(s) they displaced. This often makes the "urgent" manager reevaluate their request and be more realistic.

Leadership Needed More Than Ever Before

The managers and businesses that create the high performance work environment will be the winners of tomorrow's workplace. Management by status quo or dictatorship can have disastrous results. The responsibility for creating the high performance workplace is not the sole responsibility of just the senior executives. In fact, managers and supervisors at all levels must step outside their traditional roles and comfort zones to look at new ways of working. They have to create a work environment where people enjoy what they do, feel like they have a purpose, have pride in what they do, and can reach their potential. It requires more time, more skill, and more managers who care about people. It takes true leadership.

TD Industries in Dallas, Tex., has a unique way of making its employees feel valued and involved. One wall in the company has the photographs of all employees who have been with the company more than five years. This "equality" program goes beyond the typical slogans, posters, and HR policies. There are no reserved parking spaces for executives. Everyone uses the same bathrooms and the same water fountains. Everyone is an equal. Maybe that's why TD Industries was listed last year by *Fortune* magazine as one of the *Top 100 Best Companies*.

When former Intel executive David House became CEO of Bay Networks, he realized the troubled computer manufacturer's problems involved teaching his IT workers some basic classes. To solve the problem, he attempted to create a new culture. "Culture is what people fall back on when there are no instructions," House explained. "It gives you rules for when there are no rules and it provides a common language for moving forward."

House created four courses to teach the practices that he'd set in place at Intel: Decision-Making, Straight Talk, Managing for Results, and Effective

Meetings. He taught the courses to Bay's 120 highest-ranking executives who, in turn, taught the same courses to the other 6,000 employees.

Despite chaos for a couple of weeks, House's teachings instantly hit home and produced results. Bay reversed a $285 million loss in fiscal 1987 with $89 million in profits the first six months of fiscal 1998. Final proof was Bay's sale for $9 billion last year to Canadian telecommunications giant Nortel.

Dell Computer Corp. also has innovative work practices. Every Dell employee's job responsibility includes finding and developing their successor–not just when they are ready to move into a new role, but as an ongoing part of their performance plan.

Additionally, when Dell promotes employees, they are given fewer responsibilities, not more. "When a business is growing quickly, many jobs grow laterally in responsibility, becoming too big and complex for even the most ambitious, hardest working person to handle without sacrificing personal career development or becoming burned out," Chairman and CEO Michael Dell wrote in his book, **Direct from Dell: Strategies That Revolutionized an Industry.**

Bay and Dell each developed successful workplace programs. Some tips for setting up your own processes to help motivate your IT employees follow:

- Explain the "big picture" for the company and how this influences their employment and growth.
- Provide feedback on the employee's performance. Be specific; mention a particular situation or activity.

- Make sure they understand the company's expectations.
- Involve the employee in the decision-making process whenever possible.
- Listen to their ideas and suggestions.
- Give them room to do the job without unnecessary restrictions.
- Pay for employees to attend workshops and seminars.
- Offer on-site classes where employees can learn new skills or improve upon old ones.
- Challenge them with lots of responsibility.
- Assign them a coach or mentor to help them with development.

> **Hold Meetings Off-site:** The GSA uses off-site meetings with a facilitator to allow employees to voice complaints or air issues. Follow-up meetings resolve issues without any "backlash." As employees see results, morale goes "sky high."

Gather Your Forces: A tip from the US Air Force. The Director holds a gathering every six to eight weeks of all work forces. At that time the Director responds publicly to <u>all</u> the issues raised in suggestion boxes located throughout the work areas.

Another tip: The Director periodically gathers groups for brainstorming in areas where he is not totally familiar.

Share and Learn: At BellSouth Adv. & Publishing, they hold monthly or quarterly meetings where a representative of one department gives a 20-30 minute presentation on the work of his or her department. Employees also talk about how what each department/team does impacts the other.

Anonymous Communication: Employees with complaints about their work often choose to voice their unhappiness via an anonymous letter to the chief executive. Often ignored in the past, today executives see them as a source of possibly important information.

- At Eastman Kodak Co. (Rochester, NY) George Fisher, chairman and CEO, gives his e-mail address to everyone and receives unsigned messages every week. Multiple complaints about the same situation receive special attention based on the "where there's smoke, there's fire" attitude.

- At Browning-Ferris Industries, Inc., employees submit unsigned complaints via an open electronic forum where the system disguises the identity of the writer. Replies are posted each day on an electronic bulletin board. They screen for slanderous or redundant messages before posting.

- Rite Aid Corp. (Camp Hill, PA) decided to encourage employee input after it acquired Thrifty Payless Holdings Inc. They installed an outside voice-mail service so former Thrifty Payless employees might leave messages at any time. The service prepares verbatim transcripts for clients, thereby protecting the identity of the callers.

One word of caution: unsigned complaints may possibly open the door to future litigation because the company received notice of a problem. They also involve the risk of hurting someone's reputation, and/or spreading misinformation. It can also be difficult for managers to respond without sufficient specific information.

Chapter 7

Team Leadership TNT

Johnsonville Foods located in Sheboygan Falls, Wisconsin, has been a flagship of productivity improvement. Almost 90% of the workforce belongs to some type of team. The team, not management, decides who is hired, who is fired, who gets a pay raise. Ralph Stayer, Johnsonville's Chief Executive Officer, reports that his workers produce more sausage than he ever thought possible. His company's productivity has risen by at least 50% since 1986. Not only has productivity improved, but also teamwork has made a tremendous impact on the morale of the company.

A twelve-person team from FedEx saved the company almost $1 million in 1 1/2 years by revamping a sorting process used for overnight deliveries. Another excellent example of teamwork is Allina, a health care organization located in Minnesota. One of their teams came up with the idea saving the company $200,000 a year. They decided it was cheaper and more efficient to have hospital equipment maintained by hospital staff instead of using outside contractors. By paying close attention to this definition we gain a clear understanding of the key ingredients for team success.

> "A team is a small number of people with complementary skills who are committed to a common purpose, performance goals, and approach for which they hold themselves mutually accountable."
>
> *Jon Katzenbach and Douglas Smith, The Wisdom of Teams*

**Small Number of People**-A team usually consists of 6-12 people. Any more than this becomes difficult to manage.

**Complementary Skills**-Each person on the team possesses a particular skill or talent. When blended these talents and skills improve the capability of the team. In a high performing team, team members can perform each other's skill.

**Committed**-People do not reach maximum performance unless they are committed and trust management and each other. The human dynamic issues are critical to team success. Until team members learn to trust each other, understand each other's personalities, individual work styles, they will not become committed to the project.

**Common Purpose**-Most teams work on a particular project, task or particular type of work. Committees are not teams. The most effective teams are ones that have a written charter outlining a clear goal, purpose and mission.

**Common Approach**-You can't throw some people into a room and expect them to become an effective and productive team. Not having a structured way of doing work is one major reason teams fail. The most productive teams follow a standardized methodology for solving problems, designing a new service and/or improving a process. Initially, teams require extensive training, mentoring and coaching.

Stand-Ups: The Ritz-Carlton Hotels imitate military tradition by having "stand-ups" prior to each shift. All employees across the globe - whether at the Ritz-Carlton in Naples, Italy or the hotel in Buckhead (near Atlanta), Georgia - receive a 15 to

20 minute class on the same topic. The shift leader inspects each employee for proper uniform, nametag and appearance. The stand-up may also include questions about one of the Ritz-Carlton's 20 basics. Finally they make announcements and discuss guest preferences. Then everyone's ready to begin their shift.

Middle Managers: Unlike the US, where companies sometimes consider middle management as dead weight, Japanese companies depend on middle managers to push everyone on the team to a higher level of shared understanding. A group's knowledge base can become a major competitive advantage.

Rewarding Group Efforts: Sprint (Kansas City, Missouri) emphasizes group service goals to reduce competition among co-workers and uses both spontaneous and formal recognition programs to give awards to employee teams, manager teams or entire centers. They use call monitoring and customer feedback to identify great service. Formal awards involve financial incentives and bonuses to top-performing service employees. Other awards range from "play money" redeemable for merchandise to small parties.

Tiffany Treats: Beth Canavan, Tiffany regional vice president of retail sales, personally gives out treats each month to employees on the floors and departments that make their sales goals.

Jordan's Furniture: When the National Home Furnishings Association named Jordan's Furniture 1994 Retailer of the Year, owners Barry and Eliot Tatelman staged a fire drill so employees could see a plane pulling a "Congratulations!" banner across the sky. They use the "J-Team" concept in management and after a record setting year the owners held a surprise party for employees and their guests with the theme: "You're Simply the Best."

Pay for Performance: Actuarial Consultants, Inc. (ACI) of Bel Air, California, developed a Pay for Performance Program designed to develop teamwork and encourage employees to help make ACI profitable. The program shares profits by recognizing individual performance through a bonus pool. Bonuses are paid quarterly to all non-owner employees based on position in the firm and performance tied to individual criteria negotiated with each employee.

The Talking Stick: Try introducing the "talking stick" into your office. This idea originated from a Native American tradition. Each month a different person in the office receives the talking stick, which provides that person certain rights and privileges (which vary from office to office) for the month. For example, the "owner" could provide fellow employees one hour a month administrative leave.

Recognition and Ownership: Broderbund Software, whose products (which include Myst, Raven and Printshop) educate the world using entertainment, mystery and fun, doesn't use money to inspire employee creativity - they use *recognition and ownership.* The names of people who develop the programs are listed prominently on the packaging and displayed at the front (not the end) of the software. Broderbund employees feel that recognition is just as important as anything else. Broderbund also lets employees take chances and fail without making it a career-ending issue.

Broderbund uses a three-step development process to encourage employees to voice their ideas.

Initially a worker simply needs to convince his or her immediate boss of the idea's worthiness. Next they form a team of two to six employees and develop a product design or prototype. Then they form a focus group to assess the merit of the potential product.

New Way for United Way: United Way Campaign Goal Setting-Instead of management setting arbitrary goals, place employees on teams and allow them the freedom to set the goals. Then take it one step further and allow them to decide the reward/recognition when they reach the goal.

Buddy System: At Redken they have a buddy system for new presenters that represent our company. When a new person comes on board one of the veterans act as a coach to help them get through the tough and embarrassing times of becoming a strong presenter. They seldom want to come to their supervisor and tell them they didn't get it. It makes the coach feel empowered when the supervisor selects them. It also makes the "newbee" a better team member and it assimilates them quicker into the organization.

Club-1230: The Boys and Girls Club of America have a unique way to improve teambuilding in their Atlanta office. Expanded from once a month to once a week, they gather to meet and greet new employees and share news of the good things happening in the organization. This helps tear down silos, improves communication and makes everyone feel part of the same team.

Lunch Bunch: The Boys of Girls Club of America maintain a team approach even during lunch. Each month a group of people are appointed as the "lunch bunch." Their job is to travel around the office inviting employees to eat lunch with them. They particularly target new employees and people outside their departments. This is an excellent way to build loyalty and team spirit. Each month a new group is put on the "lunch bunch."

Great Huddle: Part of ACI's (Actuarial Consultants Inc., Bel Air, California) Pay for Performance Program includes holding short (under 30 minutes) weekly meetings - call the Great Huddle - with representatives from every department to disseminate critical numbers, review scheduling and solve problems.

Mentoring: The Defense Intelligence Agency's mentoring program allows new and junior level employees the opportunity to grow professionally. They benefit from the experience of senior level and SES personnel.

Show Some "Cheek:" In early 1997 John Briggs, director of production, felt safe when he promised salespeople at Yahoo! Inc. that he would have the Web directory's logo tattooed on his posterior when the stock passed $50 a share. However, when the stock sextupled that year, he honored his promise and had the tattoo applied--which he then displayed. However, he has declined to repeat the offer as the stock has continued to climb.

Chapter 8

Reward & Recognition TNT

We can learn a lot from the armed forces. The military gives no financial rewards for doing a good job - only a ribbon or a medal. People will do a lot for that piece of ribbon or the medal to wear on their uniform. They're meaningful and valuable because the individual **earned** them. Sometimes a person's whole status in an organization can depend on which and how many awards that person has earned.

Unfortunately, many times reward and recognition programs become meaningless if everyone gets something regardless of their performance. Here are some tips for programs that recognize and reward <u>individual accomplishments on a continuing basis</u>. An important point to remember is "immediacy" - don't wait. (Even formal programs need prompt action of some kind.)

Shoot Them A Star: J. C. Penney has an innovative program that presents employees with a 6x6 cardboard star that says, "YOU are a star performer." Details of what the person did to earn the recognition are printed on the back of the star.

"I Noticed" recognition: Have employees "notice" each other for exceptional jobs throughout the month and put names of "noticed" employees name in a box. Hold a drawing at month's end and award a $50 gift certificate to winner. Also take a photograph of the winner and post on bulletin board for everyone to see during the next month.

Kudograms: Give employees a supply of "thank you" notes (or other token of appreciation) to award to each other for doing a good job.

Standing Ovations: At S. C. Johnson Wax employees nominate fellow workers in their department for a special award. Each week the entire department stops work, goes to the awardee's cubicle or work area and gives them a "standing ovation." The person who nominated the winner presents them with a "Good Work" certificate and tells what they did to win the award.

Champion the Champion: This item is on the agenda at every meeting of JCPenney Insurance Group, which uses this verbal recognition program at departmental levels all the way to the president. At every meeting they recognize one person in honor of a special accomplishment, explain what they did and how it impacted others.

Service Over and Above Requirements (SOAR): At Nationwide Insurance, customers, managers and peers nominate employees for "service over and above." Regional six-member boards (all volunteers) meet weekly or monthly to review the nominations and select a winner. The winner selects a prize from a catalog, which includes gifts such as magnets, pins, mugs, writing pens and sweatshirts.

Spontaneous Recognition: Nationwide has also focused on spontaneous recognition. Unlike SOAR, no review process is needed to give small awards to an employee for helping a co-worker or assisting a customer "above and beyond." Spontaneous recognition awards vary from region to region and could be something like free parking for a month or simply a thank-you note.

Federal Express: Spontaneous recognition is also alive at Federal Express where managers have small budgets for day to day spontaneous reward and recognition of employee efforts through the use of such things as coupons for free sodas and chocolates. Some employees find the unexpected awards, presented in front of co-workers, more meaningful than a formal reward and recognition.

The company also has a formal awards program for excellence in customer service. They give awards when a customer compliments an employee, or an employee provides outstanding service.

Managers need awards too, and Wilfred Busby, senior manager of customer service, practices what he preaches with a catered lunch each quarter for the top performing manager and his or her group.

Other ideas from Federal Express include putting names of top-performing customer representatives in a hat for a drawing once a month. The winner gets to work their "dream shift" for a week. And give employees a "stress relief pack" consisting of silly items like Groucho Marx style glasses, a fake nose, and a bottle of soap bubbles.

Blue Ribbon Service: Katy Medical Center in Katy, Texas, uses a recognition program called Blue Ribbon Service. Employees, patients and visitors can nominate workers for a "Blue Ribbon" by filling out a card that describes what they did to deserve the award. Employees wear the blue ribbon on their clothing. For subsequent awards, they receive gold stars, or "twinkles," to attach to the ribbon. Five "twinkles" earns a permanent gold star, and five permanent stars earn the employee a gold pin.

There's also an employee-of-the-month award. Workers who've received stars are eligible as well as workers recommended by their supervisors. The award is a $25.00 gift certificate, a brass paperweight and free parking for a month. They also choose an employee of the year from among the 12 monthly winners and this person receives a $100 gift certificate and trophy.

Choose Your Own Reward: At Miami-based Creative Staffing, owner Ann Machado rewards her employees with parties, expensive dinners, chauffeured shopping sprees, spa sessions, and cooking lessons with Paul Prodhomme. She lets her employees decide what they want, then figure out how much their package costs and also how much additional business they have to generate to cover those costs. Choose your own reward - sounds like fun!

Attendance Awards: Employees of Gwinnett County (Georgia) receive perfect attendance certificates for not missing a day of work during the month. This successful program made a significant improvement in the absenteeism level among employees. It was so successful, in fact, that some employees weren't keeping doctor appointments because it would make them ineligible for the monthly award. The county recognized the unavoidable need to occasionally have appointments during the business day and instituted a second award for people who miss less than eight hours a month. This allowed employees to go to the doctor and still gave an incentive for them to take a few hours off rather than the entire day.

Zero Defects: Gwinnett County (Georgia) instituted two award programs that helped to improve the efficiency and quality of workers at the auto tag offices. The county gave a "zero defects award" to employees who during the course of a day made no errors in entering customer information. The prize: a Zero candy bar. They also instituted a "What a Difference a Day Makes" board that showed the number of people each clerk assisted. Efficiency soared as employees competed to serve the most citizens while maintaining the highest accuracy.

Free Gifts to Government Employees: Katherine Sherrington, Tax Commissioner from Gwinnett County (Georgia) wanted to award incentives and gifts to employees but had one major obstacle: no money available. Using an innovative approach, she asked local businesses if they would like to donate gifts for the cause; they said "yes."   Ms. Sherrington and her office have successfully collected quite an assortment of awards, including coffee mugs, savings bonds, calendars, clocks and umbrellas. The experience demonstrated that businesses will often freely give gifts and highlighted two special benefits: 1) It tells business people that you have a quality program and reward good work; 2) employees know the community cares about them when businesses donate the gifts.

Plus People Recognition Program: North Carolina Memorial Hospital in Chapel Hill, North Carolina, rewards employee efforts to improve patient service. Each quarter they select 12 people through peer and supervisor recommendations. Winners receive certificates and pins plus recognition through internal publicity and a celebration party in their department. At the end of the year all 48 winners enjoy an evening at a dinner theater.

Omni Hotels (Hampton, New York-based) has employee boards to select award recipients. Criteria for an award nomination include such things as making decisions outside one's area of job responsibility, promoting the hotel on one's own initiative, performing a heroic deed, working extended hours or working on a day off, etc.

A Single Rose: At one of the USAA (United States Automobile Association) centers location, whenever a service employee receives a compliment the manager goes to the employee and presents a single rose in view of all the other employees. Other approaches include handing out ribbons, reading customer letters at staff meetings, giving verbal praise and printing parts of customers' letters in the employee newsletter.

Pat on the Back: Basic American Foods uses a variation of the "Pat-on-the-Back" form to recognize employees. Any employee who sees another employee doing something good is awarded. Their form is printed on pads of yellow-stickies and placed near the employee cafeteria. The form is filled out by the nominator and placed on a special "Pat-on-the-Back" bulletin board for all to see.

Reward on the Spot! AT USG, soon after someone, such as a technician, does something innovative and the direct supervisor verifies it, they receive an award of a $50 check presented in front of their peers.

The Federal Energy Regulatory Commission also has On the Spot Awards--usually $100 cash. The Department of the Treasury offers Employer Spot Awards of $50.00.

Time-off: At the Department of the Treasury, they give "Time-Off" awards--administrative leave for special acts.

Birthday Luncheon: AT the Dept. of Treasury, a Branch Birthday Luncheon is held for employees who have a birthday that month.

Spotlight Employees: An employee at Liberty Corporation publishes a customer service newsletter on their Intranet called The Competitive Edge. It gives tips and also features a column, "The Liberty Spotlight," which focuses on new and special things and ideas in the service centers. The column includes a picture of the person in the "spotlight." The story is highlighted and posted on three physical bulletin boards in the complex.

Spirit Award: At Hill AFB (UT) they use a peer rating system that crosses organizational lines to nominate employees who have done an outstanding job. The nomination then passes through supervisory chains. Nominees who are approved receive a jacket with the base's logo and "Spirit of Hill AFB" on it.

Quiet Hero Award: Also at Hill AFB (UT), they have the "Quiet Hero Award," which is a quarterly award with nominations submitted by peers. A committee of peers evaluates and votes on the award. (Committee members serve for one year.) The Director presents a desk plaque with the "hero's" name on it to those who receive the award, and their photo is posted on the bulletin board.

Employee Recognition Breakfast: The Arkansas National Guard holds a once-a-month breakfast for all employees in the building. Teams formed from each office take turns preparing breakfast. In addition to uniting and informing employees, it is also the time for employee recognition.

Compete for Project Completion: At one maintenance department of the Defense Supply Center, individual branches compete for project completion. Projects completed 30 days ahead of schedule earn 100 points for the branch. Twenty days ahead earns 90 points, etc. Points are also used to measure quality defects and total costs. At the end of each quarter, the branch with the most points receives a trophy and a monetary award.

Peoples Choice Award: AT MCI Worldcom, each quarter everyone in the organization votes for his or her choice for the award. The winner receives a plaque and $500.00. They also give **Bravo Awards**, which are on-the-spot rewards of $50.00 and have multiple winners.

"Stars" Earn Time-Off: A tip from Shelley Sin International (Singapore): Everyone in the department sticks a "star" beside the name of another employee (in the same department) on a chart in recognition of exemplary behavior. Each month the person with the most stars receives a reward of time-off.

Say Time to "Thank You:" Warner Lambert Co., makers of Listerine mouthwash, Dentyne gum, Schick razors and Sudafed cold medicine, gave all of its 42,000 employees a Seiko watch engraved with the words, "We're making the world feel better." It was the company's way of saying thank you for their hard work and creativity in the company's turnaround.

Recognize with a Title: Employers have discovered that people do care about their job titles-- sometimes they will even choose the better title over more pay. A recent graduate with a desire to move up in a chosen career field may feel that acquiring a title which will look good on the resume is worth accepting a little less money. Recruiters have discovered that they receive a better response with well-chosen job titles. You can also encourage an employee by giving him or her a prestigious title even if you cannot afford to pay more money.

GREGORY P. SMITH

About the Author

Greg has been called a "perceptive teacher, an inspirational speaker and a motivating preacher." He specializes in showing people and businesses how to stimulate innovation, increase performance, and how to create work environments that attract, keep and motivate their workforce. His 24 years of leadership and consulting experience has helped propel him as one of America's leading authorities on employee retention, motivation and leadership.

From 2nd Lieutenant to Lieutenant Colonel, Greg built his career on the front-line as an U.S. Army Officer. When the Berlin Wall fell, he was the Director of Quality and Strategic Planning for the U.S. Army Medical Department. He was a management consultant to military generals and played a key role in the largest organizational transformation in U.S. history. Years later, his direct involvement with *"Reinventing the Government"* efforts spearheaded by the Vice President of the United States and the Army Surgeon General helped transform the military into a smaller, more customer focused organization.

He has developed and taught leadership development courses for international and national organizations including, Yamaha, Rollins, Inc., Ace Hardware, State Farm Insurance Company, AFLAC, Sweetheart Cups, Bio Lab, PacifiCare, Matrix Resources, Alltell Corporation, the U.S. Army, Advantage Rent-A-Car, the U.S. Air Force, Chicago Federal Reserve Bank, Foundation Health, Delta Airlines, Wyndham Hotels, Hallmark Cards, Service Corporation International, San Antonio School System and UNISYS.

He is listed in Harvard University's, *Profiles in Business and Management: An International Directory of Scholars and Their Research.* The *Human Resource Executive Magazine* selected him as one of the Top-Ten **"Rising Stars"** in Human Resource Management.

Greg has written numerous publications including 3 books and over 300 articles on business management. The title of his books include, *The New Leader: Bringing Creativity and Innovation to the Workplace* and *How to Attract, Keep and Motivate Your Workforce.* He also is a syndicated newspaper columnist and a regular contributor to many journals and trade magazines.

2814 Hwy. 212, SW ★ Conyers, GA 30094 ★ Tel. 770-860-9464 ★
800-821-2487 www.ChartCourse.com

Chart Your Course International

IT'S TIME FOR MORE TNT
"Tips N" Techniques"

DO YOU HAVE A SUCCESS STORY, TIP OR TACTIC THAT YOU WOULD LIKE TO SHARE?

We invite you to submit your tips or techniques that is helping to make work more fun, motivating, productive and/or more profitable.

My Tip, Technique or Story:

_____

_____

_____

_____

_____

_____

_____

_____

_____

_____

_____

_____

_____

Free Information

Send or fax me one or more of the following:

❏ I would like to subscribe to your monthly Navigator Newsletter via email. Here is my email address_____

❏ Send me the special report on how to reduce turnover and keep entry level workers.

❏ Send me your Resource Guide of your books, tools and problem-solving products.

❏ Send me information on your training programs, consulting and seminars.

❏ Send me information on your customer service training videos.

❏ We have a meeting coming up. Please send me your speakers kit.

❏ Send information on Management Development & Employee Selection Assessments.

Send to:
Name_____
Company:_____
My position:_____
Address:_____
City:_____**State**_____
Postal Code:_____**Country**_____
Phone(___)_____Fax:(___)_____
E-mail_____

Mail or fax to:
Chart Your Course International
2814 Highway 212, Conyers, Georgia 30094
770-860-9464, 800-821-2487, Fax: 770-760-0581
www.ChartCourse.com   greg@chartcourse.com

Please Visit our Website for:

- Other tools & products
- Problem-solving articles
- Newsletters
- Assessments
- New tips and ideas

www.ChartCourse.com

CHART
YOUR
COURSE
INTERNATIONAL

NOTES

NOTES

NOTES

NOTES

NOTES

NOTES

NOTES

NOTES

NOTES

NOTES